VISUAL SUPPORT FOR ACTIVITY SCHEDULES FOR EVERY DAY USE.

EASY GUIDE FOR CHILDREN, PARENTS AND THERAPIST/TEACHERS TO USE ON TABLET, CL, BLIND FOLDER, POSTER BOARD AND GAME CARDS.

LINDA RAMMLER, M.ED., PH.D., CESP
Consultant focusing on autism, positive behavior supports and inclusion
With over 40 years of experience working with people with disabilities of all ages and their families, trained and provided technical assistance to their schools, faith communities and public and private service provider agencies across the continental U.S.

I love this book for parents and their young children who have been recently diagnosed with autism or apraxia of speech! By encouraging readers to focus on people and activities of meaning for these non-verbal youngsters, this book offers readers tools to communicate with, and to teach the power of communication to non-verbal youngsters, through daily routines and rhythms grounded in nurturing family relationships. Diagnosticians and pediatricians should make this required reading for every family.

LISA GENG
President CHERAB Foundation
Communication Help, Education, Research, Apraxia
Base Conceptualist for IQed Smart Nutrition, promoting good nutrition and its effect on apraxia

"Autism Nina's First Storybook" is a "how-to" for creating a personalized storybook for children on the autism spectrum of disorders and learning disabilities. It provides a way to create a simple, personalized and highly effective alternative means of communication which reduces frustration for all concerned.

The author uses her own educational experience and expertise to help children on the autism spectrum learn to communicate and learn important life skills in a child friendly way. Beautiful and effective illustrations and rhyming repetitions, some that parents can personalize to a child's specific world, help to reinforce those words and lessons throughout the day and at bedtime. Encouraging repetition in a singsong voice helps any child with a communication impairment, but is critical to children who have communication deficits due to the motor planning impairment apraxia.

I recommend the storybook for family members, educational and speech professionals as well as a wonderful resource and an effective and simple AAC tool to have on the shelf.

KATHRYN DOYLE CHAPAR, LCSW
ABA therapist and Family Coaching and Support Specialist
Clinical social worker for over 20 years, working with children on the autism spectrum and their families

It is a wonderful, concise and encouraging guide to help everyone involved in teaching young children on the autism spectrum.

The most important task for these children is to increase communication and social interactions as well as maintain appropriate routines throughout the day. Patience, consistency, hope and trust are essential while waiting for the child to demonstrate a grasp of the skills so clearly outlined in the beautiful and appealing visuals. Being able to communicate wants, needs and feeling states greatly reduces frustration. Communication skills broaden a child's social interactions with parents, teachers, extended family members, friends, etc. The familiar people and body parts pages allow the child to show knowledge of these areas and communicate wants and needs. The picture schedule of what is happening now and what is coming next in a child's daily routine reduces anxiety about what is going to happen today and in what order.

It is a very important "how-to" book, offering a sensitive and understanding introduction for the people who interact with these inspirational children from day to day.

ODALYS ROMANO, BA, MA
Teacher of special education K-12
Teaching the handicapped for 16 years and working in developmental disabilities and special needs at United Cerebral Palsy Foundation

I really liked the book! I especially liked the step by step explanation of why a picture board/ storybook is beneficial and how to use it properly. Sadly, it is often assumed that parents already know this simply because they should.

I have used picture schedules for some of my students in the past, even those who did not have autism. Visualization is key! I love that the pictures can be viewed electronically. Technology is such a big part of our world and should also be incorporated.

My honest opinion is that it will serve as a great tool to many parents who are not sure how to get their child to communicate.

SCOTT R. DAVIS
Chief Encouragement Officer of Life (CT, USA)

I am thrilled to recommend this book helping Nina and other children who face struggles with autism and other developmental disabilities. The approach providing positive affirmations for children with disabilities is innovative. It provides families with ideas on how to create and customize their own storybook, and reminds them of the importance of having a daily routine. This helps ground the children and their families for a successful future.

Personally, I benefited from a similar learning system. When I was 5 years old, I struggled to communicate and find my place in the world due to an early onset of hydrocephalus that arrested itself. I had enduring physical and neurological shortcomings which caused developmental delays in motor function, language and social development. My parents had to find innovative ways to spark the development of language and motor function. My Mom and I created composition notebooks filled with pictures, activities and words giving me building blocks for communication.

I fully support and recommend the efforts of Mrs. Hurtado in creating her picture book and stressing the importance of a good mental attitude and a solid understanding of basic routines that will guide the disabled child through life with confidence.

ANNA GARCIA LABARBERA, LCSW

"Autism Nina's First Storybook" is a wonderful expression of the love and commitment a grandmother has for her granddaughter whose struggle with autism challenges the family as they never anticipated.

I believe that the book is a success and its goals neatly met. The instructions are clear, the visualizations are appropriate and easy to follow, and the pictures describing mood, feelings, needs and desires are well designed. The pictures are colorful without being over stimulating, and there is a game-like quality that is appealing to children. It begins the crucial process of learning how to identify and express wants and needs.

The book establishes key concepts related to daily routines and uses images and repetitive songs to help children master them. For children with learning difficulties, using visuals increases verbalization and aids the child in following daily routines using simple words and corresponding pictures for identification. "Nina's First Storybook" provides useful tools for developing and maintaining communication with young children who struggle to express themselves.

For some parents, this book can represent an important step into the complex world of developing communication. However, at its heart and what may be most useful are Hurtado's instructions for parents, urging them to not lose faith and to trust in their child's ability to surprise them. "Nina's First Storybook" is a gift from a grandmother to a granddaughter, and in turn, it helps parents develop relationships with their children founded on the simple principles of love, patience and trust.

ROSA M. RIZZO
Port Authority Police Officer/Academy Instructor
Former Director of Residence Life, NYU-Poly
Former Assistant Dean of Students, St. John's University, N.J.

Autism "Nina's First Storybook" is a well thought out, brilliantly planned "how-to" guide for children on the autism spectrum and their parents and caretakers. The author dives into the core of engaging non-verbal children by enticing them visually and using repetition as a tool to help them communicate.

This book is ground-breaking and should be used by all families that have an autistic spectrum child in their lives.

SUSAN LAVIT ROSENBERG
CEO and Founder of Mega Mouth Records Musician/Producer/Composer

I highly recommend "Autism Nina's First Storybook" for all parents of children struggling with learning disabilities. This book is an ingenious manual that clearly guides parents through the complex task of teaching children on the autism spectrum, especially when they are non-verbal. In its colorful and charming way, it becomes the perfect life tool for parents to create their own storybook and achieve success in their child's development.

Pupi Cid Hurtado, author, teacher and pioneer in Spanish Talk Show Radio in NYC, and grandmother of a beautiful, learning-challenged child, now brings her special insight to help others succeed with their childrens' life goals of functioning in the world. This book can bring about a tremendous resulting benefit. For those who use it consistently, I am confident this handbook will bring hope and help.

GRETTEL BARRANTES-QUESADA
Master in Psychology, Catholic University of San Jose, Costa Rica

Mrs. Cid-Hurtado's book aims to facilitate the interaction and communication between parents and children on the autism spectrum. She not only has theoretically investigated this spectrum, but also has a beautiful granddaughter with autism and this has made her an expert in communication with her. No doubt, this book will be of great help to parents when they receive the diagnosis and they are confused and overwhelmed, not knowing how to start communicating with their child.

Copyright © 2013 Pupi Cid Hurtado

All rights reserved including the right of reproduction in whole or in part in any form.
Published by Pupi Cid Hurtado

www.autismbookandthings.com
Contact pupicidhurtado@gmail.com

Quantity discounts are available, contact the publisher at above address.

Library of Congress Cataloging-in-Publication Data 2017945878
Pupi Cid Hurtado

Autism
Nina's First Story Book
How to Do Your Child's Storybook

English

ISBN-13 978-0-9990869-0-2

First printing 2017
Printed in the United States of America

NINA'S FIRST STORYBOOK
HOW TO DO YOUR CHILD'S STORYBOOK

Nina

With Gratitude to...

My beautiful Nina, my love, teacher, inspiration and joy and to all
beautiful children like Nina and their parents,
To God our Creator, who sent us His angels so we may evolve
in love and care as our mission,
Nina's parents, Mike and Raquel Meehan and Nina's sisters, Natalia Ines
and Paloma Bella, for loving and caring so much for Nina,
My daughter, Carmen Pia, for her encouragement and support
My husband, Mark, for his unconditional support
Enrique Vignolo, for his talent and support

Created by: Pupi Cid Hurtado   Illustrated by: Enrique Vignolo

INTRODUCTION

I am Nina's grandmother. Nina is a playful, smiling, smart and beautiful 12 year old girl on the autism spectrum. Nina is non verbal (oral apraxia) and suffers from completely spontaneous and complex seizures. In my desire to help Nina, I want to help all the beautiful children on the spectrum by writing a story book using the words she is learning in school. Her parents help to reinforce those words at bedtime and during the day with beautiful illustrations and a series of rhyming repetitions.

It is my greatest desire to help Nina and all the children who suffer from this mysterious condition of autism and other nonverbal learning disorders. This is where I came up with the idea in my mind, (because of the inspiration that comes from Love), to create a book that serve as "Model" so that parents can copy and thus, reinforce in the house the words they teach in school, and they can do it in a pleasant, practical, simple and attractive way.

Nina has given me my first encouraging critique of the book. When she saw it, her eyes were avidly looking for the right illustration she wanted to point to. When I asked her, "what do you want Nina?" she pointed to "I want to eat" and "I am hungry." Then she pointed that she was "happy".

When I showed Nina the book and saw her use it to communicate effectively, I saw that my vision for this book was truly going to help her and children like her to communicate.

THE REASON OF THE BOOK

Children who are on the autism spectrum are usually very visual learners and have a great memory. The goal of this book is to first help identify words and routines, and then ultimately master them. I have learned that using "visuals" increases verbalization and helps the child to follow daily routines by using simple words and corresponding pictures for identification. For this reason, the illustrations are very important for them to identify the action and understand what they are being told with words alone. When you speak to the child, do it slowly, clearly and one word at a time. This gives them time to process and understand it. This repetition is critical to the child's success.

When children are visually taught the routine they follow and are spoken to at the same time, the mental process and learning becomes easier for them. Visuals will also help parents to be consistent in maintaining these skills by reinforcing the teachings from the child's school. The child not only learns but has less frustration and less anxiety while acquiring more security through the structure of communicating more effectively.

The "continuity and persistence" is important in everything to give them structure. The goal of this book is to serve as a "model" for parents to create their own books using photos of their child in different situations, moments and routines to personalize their own book making their child their own model. This "model" book will help you start creating your own stories and visual guides which will help the child move through the day with less frustration and anxiety. The parents can use their child's name as the main character sharing a pleasant moment between the parents and child.

Each of these pages, have been studied and using Nina as a critic of it, putting the soul and heart in prayer for the book to be effective. With a lot of love for Nina and for the children like Nina. Desiring that all the potential that they have inside, can be developed and they can come forward all the beauty, the Gifts and skills that God in His infinite Love has given each one of them when they were created. "God only sends special children to special parents," because he knows, that these parents will take care of and love that Pure Angel, that He gives them. One day, we will realize this truth. These children, in addition, will be our "Crowns" in heaven.

STRUCTURE OF THE BOOK

Page One. "Hi, my name is!" and it may be helpful to paste a picture of your child there. On the second and third squares, paste the pictures of the mother and father. The rest of the squares can be used for siblings, grandparents, teachers, doctors, or anyone the child regularly encounters with their names written below their pictures. Use this page frequently so the child will associate the faces with their respective names.

Page Two. The "Good Morning!" page can be placed in the bathroom. Cut out the last two pictures at the bottom and put them in a convenient place. When using them, show and point to them by saying "first breakfast and then rinse your mouth." Or "backpack, soon the school bus is here." This provides confidence and less anxiety in the morning.

Page Three. "I Am" page you may say, "How are you feeling?" and read, "I am happy" etc. Show your child as you point to each picture and say the name of the feeling. Give him time to look at and get familiar with each picture. Soon he may start to recognize his feelings and respond to your question by pointing and repeating it after you.

Page Four and Five. " I want this". In there pages, you will also help point out each drawing so that the child can communicate what they want weather it is a snack or a bath.

Page Six. "Going home". This page is a guide to the routine that the child should follow back home, always using the routine with consistency.

Page Seven. This is a guide to train your child and make it a habit to go to the bathroom. This group of repeated words should be said with rhythmic intonation, to make the training entertaining, while the child is seated. It is recommended to take the child every 30 minutes on the clock and sit them down on the toilet and entertain them with singing words until he makes his needs. This training must have discipline and do it every 30 minutes until your child recognize and get used to this routine. With consistency you will have the desired and necessary sucess.

Page Eight. "I want to". Ask the child what he needs and point to the action for him to copy and communicate what he wants.

Page Nine. It's another guide to teach him how to pick up after playing. "Give Me" to teach him to ask for something. "Help Me" teach him to ask for help.

Page Ten. "We Go To" children feel safe when they know what to expect, children with autism need this security. When they are shown where they are going, they feel less anxious, and are much easier to cooperate with.

Page Eleven. "Body Parts" To teach him the body parts, touching each part of his body as each illustration points. You can also make two copies to play cards for the child to match body parts.

Page Twelve. "Wait and Take Your Turn" repeat words to say with rhythmic intonation. It is important to teach them to wait their turn when they play. In this way they are taught respect and order for life in society.

Page Thirteen. It teaches them the "safety symbols" they should know. Repeat the words rhythmically.

Page Fourteen and Fifteen. "Meal Time and Night Time" The illustrations will be used in the sequence according to the custom of the house. Always point with your fingers and show the child each step. When going to bed, never forget to tell your child "I love you a lot" "You are great" because these phrases will be the last thing you have left in their subconscious before going to sleep. These phrases will help the child to feel accepted and loved and will raise their self-esteem which will help to overcome any condition that the child has.

Remember this: "Practice, practice, practice! Patience, patience, patience!" In the remaining pages, try to read the word groups rhythmically and like a little song. For example "wash your hands" or from the "safety rules" page, "Walk, Walk, Walk," "Stop, Stop, Stop." As you read those action verbs rhythmically, they become catchy songs easier to learn than written lessons.

The illustrations in this book can be used in sequence or rearranged as you need them. Say "show me," and guide the child through the pictures by repeating the name of each picture until the child discovers what he wants. Guide the child's finger to the selected picture as you repeat the name of the word or action desired. You can also cut the illustrations and make cards to use them as a game, change the sequence of the schedules, etc. Use this book as a sample to do your own book! Personalize the story using your child's name and his pictures and his routines. It will help him relate better if you use the visuals to make it into his own personal storybook. Copy each page and laminate them, then place them in specific places. You can also view the pictures on your Tablet, or cell phone when you're away from home. Even though your child may not have much patience or attention, you should sound excited, happy and rhythmic. Don't give up, even if your heart is really asking, "when will my child be engaged?" Have courage and faith that your child will surprise you someday.

Repetition and consistency are the keys for your dear child's success. Patience is the key to your success, and you WILL succeed!

With my love to all those beautiful children and my admiration and encouragement to their parents, Pupi

CONTENTS

Hi, my name is 1

Good morning! 2

I am 3

I want this 4-5

Back home 6

Potty time 7

I want to 8

Put in, put on, give me, help me 9

We go to 10

Body parts 11

Take your turn 12

Walk and stop 13

Meal time 14

Night time 15

Notes 16-18

Good morning!

Toothpaste on brush

Brush teeth

Rinse your mouth

Wash face

Brush hair

Get dressed

Breakfast time

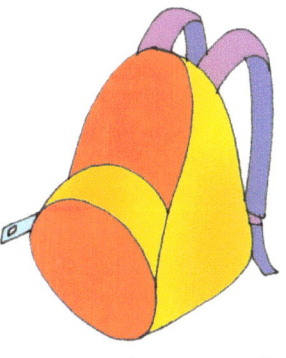
Backpack

School bus

I am

Happy Sad Angry
Hungry Hot
Cold Sleepy Not feeling well

I want this

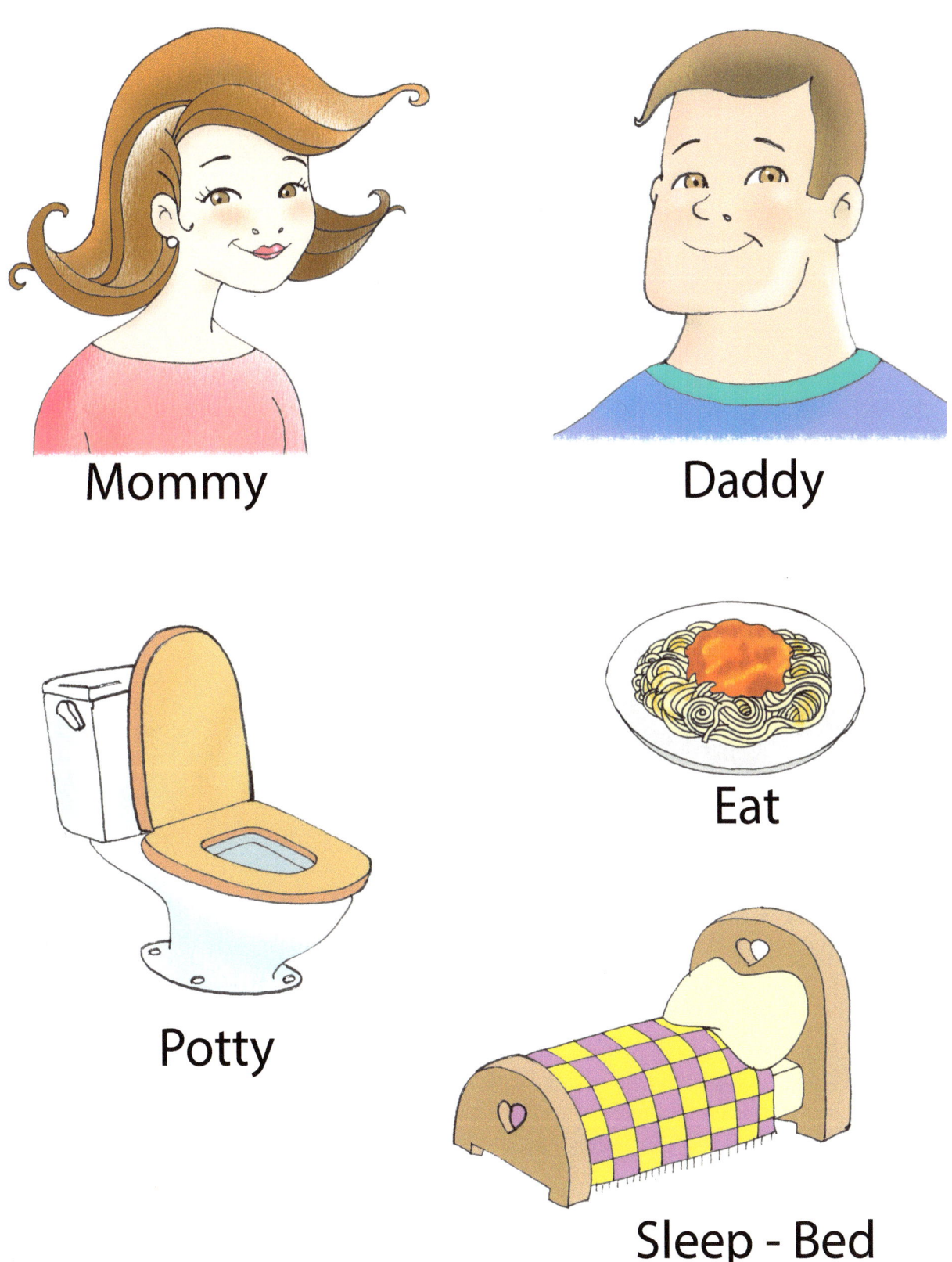

I want this

Relax

Snack  Bath

Play - Swing  Swim

Water

Back home

Hang coat and backpack

Wash your hands

Potty

Snack

Read a book

Potty time

Pants down, pants down, down, down!

Potty, poop! Poop, poop, poop, poop!

Clean up, clean up, clean up!

Pants up, pants up, pants, up!

Flush, flush, flush!

Wash hands, wash hands, wash hands!

I want to

Go outside - Take a walk

Park - play

Play music

Car - Ride

Piano

Guitar

Cook

Tablet

Computer

Keyboard - To Type

Paint

Favorite dvd

Put in, put on, give me, help me

Put in

Put on

Give me

Help me

We go to

Restaurant　　　Shopping　　　Doctor

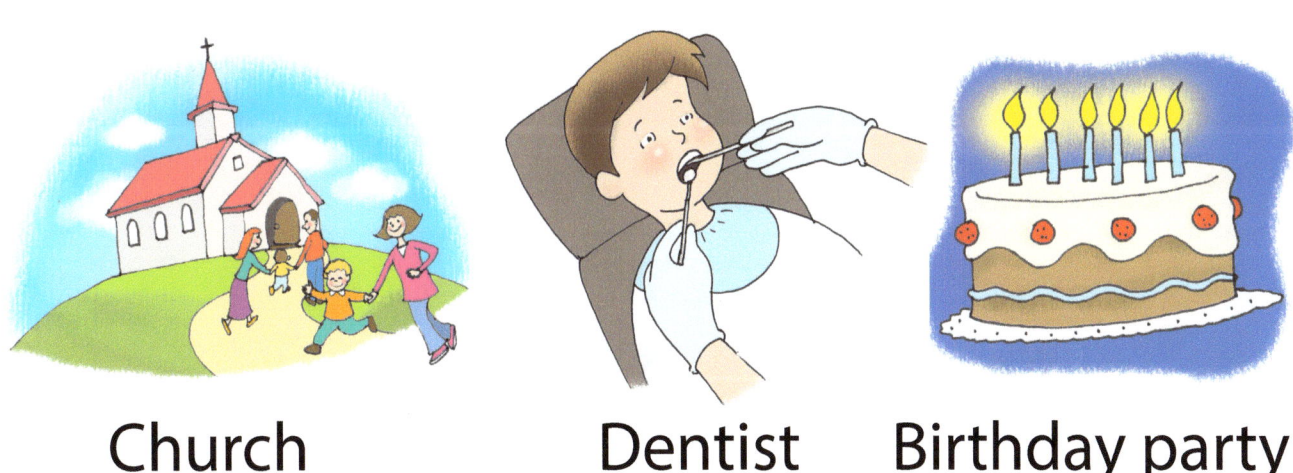

Church　　　Dentist　　　Birthday party

Library　　　School　　　Home

Body parts

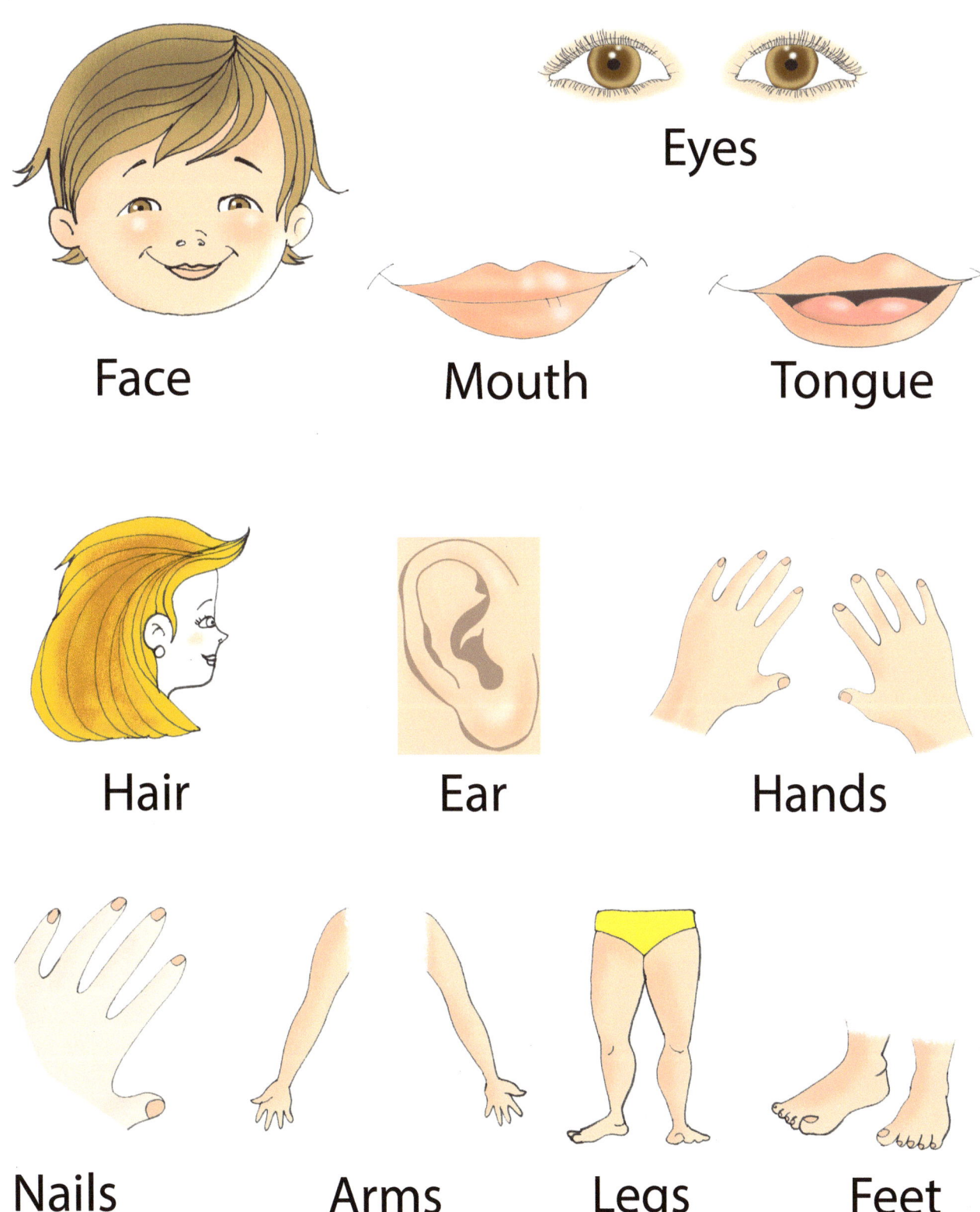

11

Take your turn

Wait and take your turn. Take your turn, take your turn! Wait and take your turn.

Walk and stop

Walk. Walk, walk,
walk, walk,
walk, walk, walk,
walk!

Stop. Stop, stop,
stop, stop,
stop, stop, stop, stop!

Walk. Walk, walk, walk!

Stop. Stop, stop, stop!

Meal time

Meal time

More!

All done!

Wipe your mouth

Night time

Brush teeth

Take a bath

Put on pajamas

Bed time, goodnight! I love you.

NOTES

NOTES

Recent Update on Nina's progress

Nina progresses day by day in understanding and learning. She is blooming like a flower!

She works very hard every day with therapists and teachers. She takes dance classes once a week and learned to follow the movements. She learned how to dress and undress herself, and to prepare her sandwiches and snacks for her school lunch. She swims like a pro and also knows how to manage her tablet to see her favorite cartoons and family pictures. When she sees family pictures, she shows emotions and kisses photos of her mother and father. She is learning how to type with SOMA and Facilitated Communications methods, and she is texting with her older sister. They show that she is witty and funny, with a bright mind and incredible intelligence!

She typed that she won't be able to do things she would like to do because she is on the autism spectrum and her body does not help her and frustrates her even when she types. She also said she has tantrums because she can't express what she wants or feels. She mentions that she has bad days and sad days, and asks if that happens to boys too.

She likes science, and picks out clothing she would like to wear. Nina also asks what is "after life" and what is heaven like? She typed, she did not want "Abuela" (me) to die because I am her best friend. It melted my heart!!! I could write a book about Nina's progress and typing!

I wish I could send some of her typing to the doctors who gave us the overwhelming and sad diagnosis of autism resulting in retardation and sent us home with little hope.

Dear mothers and dear fathers and grandparents, let me tell you that there IS hope for our children on the spectrum. With appropriate therapies, hyperbaric chamber treatments, supplements, proper diet, exposing them to dancing, swimming, sports, music, and all kind of therapies, you can give them a life.

Celebrate and encourage them at every milestone to help raise their self-esteem. Do it even when they seem to not pay attention. Never speak negatively about them and never, in front of them. The best medicine is showing them how much you love them because they need to feel they are loved. I am speaking to you based on our experience with Nina. Every child on the spectrum is different, but they are all human beings with feelings and potential, and all of them have very special gifts.

The process is challenging and heart breaking, but you will grow along with your child. I like to recommend to you to read books that will inspire and encourage you. Among others, from Temple Grandin, William Stillman, and Tito Rajarshi Mukhopadhyay (his mother created the SOMA Communications system).

May God bless you and your child as He has blessed us with Nina!

www.ingramcontent.com/pod-product-compliance
Lightning Source LLC
Chambersburg PA
CBHW060822090426

42738CB00002B/73